FIRST THINGS, LAST THINGS

A *Cass Canfield* BOOK

Books by Eric Hoffer

Eric Hoffer

FIRST THINGS, LAST THINGS

HARPER & ROW, PUBLISHERS
NEW YORK, EVANSTON, SAN FRANCISCO
LONDON

1817

23692

1

Man's
Most Useful
Occupation

It is a story worth retelling. In 1879 the Spanish amateur archaeologist Marquis de Sautuola and his little daughter Maria discovered the breathtaking paintings of bison and other animals on the ceiling of the cave at Altamira. The Marquis was forty-eight years old, sparely built, reticent, not strikingly original, but with a consuming hunger for distinction. It was actually little Maria who discovered the paintings. The Marquis did what other prehistorians were doing at the time: he dug and puttered just inside the entrance of the cave, looking for stone tools, bone needles and pieces of carved mammoth ivory. But the twelve-year-old Maria, who held the torch to give light to the Marquis, strayed some distance from the entrance, and waving the torch playfully over her head she suddenly saw a herd of bison galloping on the ceiling, and cried out, "Toros! toros!"

The Marquis recognized immediately the significance of the discovery for prehistory and for himself. Here was a heaven-sent chance to land him in one jump in the front ranks of prehistorians. He was going to write a monograph on the paintings, magnificently illustrated, and the name of Sautuola would forever mark an epochal change in our conception of Paleolithic man.

Everything went swimmingly for a while. The Marquis wrote to his friend Professor Vilanova of the University of Madrid. The professor came, saw the paintings, and was swept off his feet. The Madrid newspapers had front-page stories and photographs of the momentous discovery. King Alfonso XII visited the cave and stayed at the Marquis's castle in Santillana del Mar. The Marquis also had a painter. He had some time earlier befriended a destitute French painter, afflicted with dumbness, who had been stranded in the neighborhood, and he now put him to making the sketches for his treatise.

Then disaster struck out of the blue. At the congress of prehistory in Lisbon in 1880 the assembled experts and scholars denied the authenticity of the Altamira paintings. Professor Emile Cartailhac of the University of Toulouse thought it was all a hoax perpetrated by the Marquis to obtain cheap renown and make fools of the experts. Anti-Altamira articles began to appear in the press. Professor Vilanova eventually went over to the experts. The Marquis tried again at the next congress, held in Algiers in 1882. No one would listen to him. The Marquis retired to his estates and died in 1888 at the relatively early age of fifty-seven.

The dénouement is interesting. Fifteen years after the death of the Marquis, Professor Emile Cartailhac of the University of Toulouse published a beautifully illustrated monograph on the paintings under the title "La Caverne d'Altamira."

2

The story is told here not to demonstrate the fallibility of experts. Actually the experts could not help themselves. These paintings supposedly done by Paleolithic savages who lived fifteen to thirty thousand years ago had nothing primitive, crude or awkward about them. They were masterpieces, and closer to the feeling and understanding of modern man than any ancient art. Moreover, the other colors, deep reds and the blackest black, were vivid and fresh, and felt damp to the touch. It was natural to suspect that the paintings were the work of a living painter—probably of the French painter in the Marquis's employ.

Equally crucial was the picture the experts had of the

Paleolithic savage. He was more primitive than most of
the global dropouts who make up the present-day primitive tribes in various parts of the world—at least as
primitive as the Australian aborigines. Paleolithic man
had only the most rudimentary tools. He could not
make a pot, weave cloth or work metals. He had no
domesticated animals, not even a dog. What connection
could there be between such an utterly primitive crea-
ture and works of art which are among the greatest
achievements of mankind?

We know that eventually the experts changed their
minds about the paintings. Was this due to a drastic
revision of their thought on the nature and life of early
man? Not that you can notice it. Pick up an armful of
books on prehistoric man and you still find the Paleolithic hunter depicted as wholly absorbed in a perpetual,
cruel struggle for sheer survival; always only one step
ahead of starvation, always facing the problem of how
to eat without being eaten, never knowing when he fell
asleep whether he would be there in the morning. Why
then the paintings? They were, we are told, an aid in
the eternal quest for food; they reflect the deep anxiety
of the hunter community about the animals on whose
meat they depended for very life; they were part of the
magical rites connected with the capture and killing of
game. The savage, we are told, had noticed that by imi-
tating, by disguising himself as an animal, he could lure

and kill his prey, which led him to believe that likeness was the key to mysterious powers by which to control other creatures. The more lifelike the likeness the greater the magic. Hence the marvelous realism of the paintings.

3

Now, one can admit the magical connotations of the cave paintings and yet reject the suggestion that Paleolithic art had its origin in magic. Giotto and Michelangelo painted for the church and many of their paintings had a magical purpose, but no one would maintain that religion was at the root of the impulse, drive, preoccupation and aspiration which animated these artists. We know that the shaman, medicine man and priest make use of the artist; they subsidize him and enable him to execute momentous works. But magic and religion do not bring forth the artist. The artist is there first. The Paleolithic artists engraved, carved, and modeled in clay long before they executed the animal frescoes in the caves. The artistic impulse is likely to emerge where there are leisure, a fascination with objects, and a delight in tinkering and playing with things.

The first thing I do when I get a book on prehistoric man is go to the index to see whether it has the word *play*. It is usually not there. You find Plato but not play.

First Things, Last Things

The experts take it for granted that man's ability to master his environment was the product of a grim, relentless struggle for existence. Man prevailed because he was more purposeful, determined and cunning than other creatures. Yet, whenever we try to trace the origin of a skill or a practice which played a crucial role in the ascent of man, we usually reach the realm of play.

Almost every utilitarian device had its ancestry in a non-utilitarian pursuit or pastime. The first domesticated animal—the dog puppy—was not the most useful but the most playful animal. The hunting dog is a rather late development. The first domesticated animals were children's pets. Planting and irrigating, too, were probably first attempted in the course of play. It is also plausible that the wheel, the sail, brickmaking, etc. were invented in the course of play. The Aztecs did not have the wheel, but some of their animal toys had rollers for feet. Ornaments preceded clothing. The bow, we are told, was a musical instrument before it became a weapon. Man first used clay to mold figurines rather than make pots.

Seen thus it is evident that play has been man's most useful occupation. It is imperative to keep in mind that man painted, engraved, carved, modeled long before he made a pot, wove cloth, worked metals or domesticated an animal. Man as an artist is infinitely more ancient than man as a worker. Play came before work, art before production for use. Pressing necessity often prompted man to make use of things which amuse. When grubbing for necessities man is still in the animal kingdom. He becomes uniquely human and is at his creative best when he expends his energies, and even risks his life, for that which is not essential for sheer survival. Hence it is reasonable to assume that the humanization of man took place in an environment where nature was bountiful, and man had the leisure and the inclination to tinker and play. The ascent of man was enacted in an Eden-like playground rather than on a desolate battleground.

4

Let us return to the Paleolithic hunters who painted the cave masterpieces. Was their life an endless cruel struggle for sheer survival? Actually they lived in a hunter's paradise, a crossroad of the seasonal migrations of huge herds of bison, reindeer, wild horses, musk ox and deer. The animals filed past in their thousands along well-defined routes. Food was almost no problem. The hunters lived mostly in skin tents and were clad in sable, arctic fox and other fancy furs. Judged by their fine bone needles the Paleolithic hunters were expert tailors. They sported swagger sticks of mammoth ivory beautifully carved and engraved. They wore necklaces of shell and perforated animal teeth, and engraved pendants made of ivory, bone, horn or baked clay. They were sportsmen, their life rich with leisure yet not without tensions and passionate preoccupations. They had leisure to develop and exercise subtle skills not only in carving, engraving and painting, but also in elaborating the sophisticated art of fishing with bone fishhooks and sinew lines. They probably had secret societies which met in cave hideouts adorned with engravings and paintings of animals. The shaman injected himself into these sporting activities and gradually endowed them with a pronounced magical connotation.

I said that the artistic impulse is likely to arise where there is a fascination with objects. In the case of the Paleolithic hunter the objects were animals. Almost all the engravings, carvings and paintings of Paleolithic man were of animals. What was his attitude toward animals? He adored and worshiped them. They were his betters. Man among the animals is an amateur among superbly skilled and equipped specialists, each with a built-in tool kit. Man has neither claws nor fangs nor horns to fight with, neither scales nor hide to shield him, no special adaptations for burrowing, swimming, climbing or running. He craved the strength, speed and skill of the superior animals around him. When he boasted he likened himself unto an elephant, a bull, a deer. He watched the adored animals with the total absorption of a lover, and could paint them in vivid detail even on the ceiling of a dark cave.

Man's being an unfinished, defective animal has been the root of his uniqueness and creativeness. He is the only animal not satisfied with being what he is. His ideal was a combination of the perfections he saw in the animals around him. His art, dances, songs, rituals and inventions were born of his groping to compensate himself for what he lacked as an animal. His spirituality had its inception not in a craving to overcome his animality but in a striving to become a superior animal. In the cave of Trois Frères the sorcerer painted high on a ledge above the ground seems to rule over the world of animals depicted on the walls below, and this sorcerer, whose face is human, is a composite of animals: he has the antlers of a stag, the ears of a wolf, the eyes of an owl, the paws of a bear, the tail of a horse, and the genitalia of a wildcat.

5

The most crucial consequence of man's incurable unfinishedness is of course that he cannot truly grow up. Man is the only perpetually young thing in the world, and the playground is the ideal milieu for the unfolding of his capacities and talents. It is the child in man that is the source of his uniqueness and creativeness.

I have always felt that five is a golden age. We are all geniuses at the age of five. The trouble with the juvenile is not that he is not yet a man but that he is no longer a child. If maturing is to have meaning it must be a recapturing of the capacity for total absorption and the avidity to master skills characteristic of a five-year-old. But it needs leisure to be a child. When we grow up the world steals our hours and the most it gives us in return is a sense of usefulness. Should automation rob us of our sense of usefulness, the world will no longer be able to steal our hours. Banned from the marketplace we shall return to the playground and resume the task of learning and growing. Thus to me the coming of automation is the coming of a grand consummation, the completion of a magic circle. Man first became human in an Eden playground, and now we have a chance to attain our ultimate destiny, our fullest humanness, by returning to the playground.

2

The Birth
of Cities

It has been generally assumed that the birth of the city came at the culmination of a technological revolution which took place in Mesopotamia between 4000 and 3000 B.C. The late Professor V. Gordon Childe,* a foremost authority on the prehistory of the city, maintained that not only the domestication of plants and animals but also the invention of the wheel, sail, plow, irrigation, brickmaking, metallurgy, the calendar, and even the invention of writing preceded the coming of the city. It was assumed that all these momentous inventions and discoveries were made in the sticks, in some rudimentary settlements or villages.

To anyone even vaguely acquainted with the nature

* *What Happened in History* (Pelican Books A108); *Man Makes Himself* (Mentor Books M64).

of the creative situation such an assumption will seem absurd. Whoever heard of anything new coming out of a village! All through the millennia the village has been a bastion of deadly conservatism. Even at this moment, in many parts of the world, villages are still stuck in the Neolithic Age. A crucial characteristic of present-day backward, stagnant countries is that the village and not the city is the basic unit of society. People who live close to nature have little occasion to experience continuous progress toward something new and better. They are immersed in the endless recurrence of similar events. The village is equally inhospitable to strange people and strange ways.

From the point of view of the creative milieu it is difficult to see how the subtly creative act of plant domestication was conceived in the sticks and, as most prehistorians believe, by food-collecting women driven by the necessity to stave off starvation. The creative milieu is characterized not only by a considerable degree of leisure and the absence of pressing necessity, which stifles the impulse to tinker and play, but also by the interaction of people with different ways and bents. Where in any village can you find a human situation distantly approaching such a milieu?

It has long been taken for granted that the farming village preceded the city; that the earliest village must be far more ancient than the earliest city, and that some villages grew into cities. When some years ago Kathleen Kenyon at Jericho and James Mellaart at Catal Hüyük unearthed walled cities which antedated by several millennia any excavated ancient village they upset many archaeological applecarts. Indeed, Miss Kenyon suggested that the breakthrough from food collecting to food production took place in walled cities like Jericho.* At Çatal Hüyük the presence of wall paintings of hunting scenes and of large hunting weapons suggested to Mr. Mellaart that here was a link between the fabulous hunter-cave-painters of the upper Paleolithic and the new order of food production.†

2

Domestication of seed plants was first achieved in the Near East after the end of the last Ice Age. There is no evidence that the melting of the ice cap in Europe and other northern latitudes about 10,000 B.C., which brought about poignant changes in the life of the Paleolithic hunters, caused crucial climatic changes in the lands of the fertile crescent. In other words, domestication of plants did not come as a response to climatic change. Climatic conditions in the Near East were prob-

* Kathleen M. Kenyon, *Digging Up Jericho* (New York: Frederick A. Praeger, 1957).
† James Mellaart, *Çatal Hüyük* (New York: McGraw-Hill, 1967).

ably as favorable for the growth of seed plants before 10,000 B.C. as they were after. Nor was domestication prompted by a shrinkage of the food supply. The abundance of wild barley, wheat and other edible grasses made the Near East an ideal place for intensive grain collecting. Some time ago, the American archaeologist Jack R. Harlan tested the harvesting of wild grain on a mountainside in southern Turkey. He used a reconstructed sickle with a flint blade. He estimated that "a family group beginning harvesting near the base of the mountain and working slowly upslope as the season progressed, could easily collect over a three week span, without ever working too hard, more grain than the family could possibly consume in a year."* There is no reason to assume that conditions were substantially different in prehistoric days. Moreover, hunting with bow and arrow was a long-established practice among Near Eastern food collectors and, judging by the enormous quantities of gazelle bones, a highly rewarding one. In short, domestication of plants was first attempted by people living in an economy of plenty.

What then was the event after 10,000 B.C. which prompted expert grain collectors living in a region rich in wild grains to plant the seed they had in their leather pouches and storage bins? Something momentous must

* *Archaeology*, Vol. 20, No. 3 (June, 1967), p. 197.

have happened in the Near East a millennium or so after the melting of the ice cap in Europe. One ought to look for traces of some upheaval that shattered and churned the long-established communes of grain collectors and threw their human debris together in places of refuge where pressed against each other and with time on their hands they talked, reflected, tinkered and experimented. It was probably in such a stockade or sanctuary that grain production was first conceived and attempted.

What could have been the cause of such an upheaval?

3

In Europe, the end of the last Ice Age had dramatic effects. The herds of migratory bison, reindeer, wild horse and mammoth, already decimated by a continuously perfected hunting technique, disappeared completely. The land, free of ice, was soon covered with forest hospitable only to smaller solitary animals, such as deer and boar, which had to be hunted with bow and arrow. The hunters had to become food collectors living on these smaller animals and on fish, shellfish and berries. The shift from the communal hunt of large game to food collecting drained life of fierce joys, sharp exertions, instinctual satisfactions and the exhilaration of communion. It is not at all unreasonable to assume that the proudest and most venturesome among the hunters began to drift eastward and southward in search of a new hunters' paradise.* Such a migration of hunters would be neither anomalous nor unprecedented since we know of migrations even during the Ice Age when man first reached Australia and North America. Sometime in the ninth millennium the drifting bands of hunters reached the Near East, where they came up against the territorial rights of long-established, thriving communes of grain collectors. The resulting clash and protracted struggle must have been the event which set the stage for the invention of domestication.

The full emergence of agriculture may have been a slow evolution. But the idea of domestication came probably as a sudden illumination. Both the grain collectors and the hunter bands sought refuge in walled places near wells or rivers. These stockades were embyronic cities, where a mixed group of people, the debris of various communes, had the leisure, between forays to collect food and harass the enemy, to talk, tinker, and eventually hit upon the idea of producing food by planting grain in plots of ground.

It is of absorbing interest that the art of earliest Jericho and of Çatal Hüyük should call to mind the hunter-cave-painters of the Late Paleolithic. It shows a naturalism and a refinement not found in other food-collecting

* The Persian word *Pairidaize* means a hunting preserve.

[20]

areas. In Europe, Asia and North Africa the art of the food-collecting period is typified by schematic figures of animals and human beings, and abstract geometric patterns, with not a trace of the superb realism which animated the Paleolithic cave paintings. In addition to the art there were also large hunting weapons and burial customs to indicate some continuity between the Paleolithic hunters and the postglacial Near East.

4

Earliest Jericho was a sanctuary adjacent to a copious well. It was occupied by hunters who made it a more or less permanent camping place. Some of the clay floors had stone sockets for the placing of totem poles. There is evidence of the tentative beginning of agriculture dating from 8840 B.C. The presence of Anatolian obsidian indicates a link with northern regions.

The settlement grew rapidly in size during the eighth millennium and was heavily fortified with three superimposed dry-stone walls, a huge watchtower with an internal staircase, and a deep rock-cut ditch outside the wall.

Toward the end of the eighth millennium Jericho was taken over by a different cultural group, possibly by the one against whom the massive fortifications had been erected. There is evidence that the city was deserted for a time previous to the takeover. The newcomers raised crops and domesticated the goat. Though they had no pottery, they knew how to make clay figurines of the Mother Goddess, and how to plaster skulls and mold them into faces of singular beauty. They fashioned beautiful stone vessels.

There is no telling whether the first settlers were natives or invading hunters. The fact that some were longheaded and some broadheaded may indicate a mixed population. Nor do we know whether the people who took over Jericho after the end of the eighth millennium, and who were more artistically gifted, were of the invading Paleolithic hunters. It is perhaps legitimate to assume that the first attempt to plant grain was made by grain collectors familiar with the life cycle of wild grain plants, and that the hunters appropriated the practice from them. One ought also to assume that the hunters from the north would not readily take to the life of an agriculturalist. Many of them would sooner or later turn northward again and resume the search for a hunter's paradise. They would carry with them the new mode of food production, and a taste for living in a fortified city. It was probably such remnants of the Paleolithic hunters who built the city of Çatal Hüyük on the Konya plain in Anatolia.

Çatal Hüyük was a town of substantial size in the

seventh millennium B.C., three or four thousand years before the famous cities of Mesopotamia. The dwellers of the town farmed and hunted. Since the Konya plain had no wild grain plants, the agriculture of Çatal Hüyük was imported from somewhere else, probably from Palestine, as Mr. Mellaart conjectures.

As late as 6000 B.C. the Konya plain teemed with wild life. There were aurochs, wild pig, several species of deer, two species of wild ass, wild sheep and some gazelle. The people of Çatal Hüyük made good use of the hunter's paradise. They also cultivated no less than fourteen food plants, and raised sheep and goats. Since the houses were built one against the other, the city presented to the outside world a blank wall which gave it the appearance of a fortress.

As already mentioned, the upper Paleolithic heritage is clearly recognizable in Çatal Hüyük. There are the large hunting weapons, the realistic hunting scenes painted on walls, the modeling of animals wounded in hunting rites, the practice of red-ocher burials and, finally, certain types of stone tools.

5

It is safe to assume that there were other early cities, foci of the earliest civilization. They lasted for millennia, but for some unknown reason were abandoned late in the sixth millennium B.C. It was then (about 5000 B.C.) that drab farming villages began to dot the Near East. The prototype of the village was probably a suburb housing the dropouts who could not make it in the early city. When the city disappeared the suburb continued as a village. The agricultural villages were, then, the end product of the decay of the first cities.

It is in areas where the remnants of cities are more ancient than the remnants of farming villages that domestication originated. Where cities are a late development, as in Egypt, Europe and elsewhere, domestication was introduced from without.

The idea of two cycles of city building separated by several millennia is not as strange as it sounds. There are instances in history of precursors foreshadowing a momentous event long in advance. Thus the voyages of the Vikings, beginning in the eighth century, were forerunners of the voyages of discovery in the fifteenth and sixteenth centuries. Though there is no unquestionable evidence that Columbus benefited from the experience of the Vikings, there is no doubt that the Sumerians, who initiated the second cycle of city building in the fourth millennium, made full use of the agriculture and the crafts elaborated in the earliest cities and conserved in the villages of Mesopotamia. In the Sumerian language the words for farmer, herdsman, fisherman, plow,

smith, carpenter, weaver, potter, mason and perhaps
even merchant are non-Sumerian.

The Sumerians were hunters who came into lower
Mesopotamia, from the mountainous region to the north-
east, sometime in the fourth millennium. We are so used
to the idea that the village was a preliminary to the city
that we assume the villager to have a greater affinity to
city life than the hunter. Actually, the life of a band
of hunters has many things in common with life in the
city: adventurous vicissitudes, fabulous windfalls, meet-
ings with strangers, ceaseless movement and ceaseless
vying, and the exhilaration of communion. The drab
Neolithic village was without the breath of freedom,
and the human spirit lost there its swing and extrava-
gance. Neolithic agriculture brought the curse of work
to man and animal. Only in the city did the human spirit
regain for a time the flight it knew in the Eden playground of the Paleolithic hunters. Moreover, no one
doubts that the trader who is most at home in the city
has in him more of the hunter than of the villager.
Finally, the hunter's talent for organization places him
way above the villager as a potential city builder. Hence
often in history hunters have played a decisive role in
the birth of cities. Aztec civilization was a fusion between that of the native Toltecs, skilled in crafts, and
that of the invading Aztec hunter-warriors, skilled in
organization. The word Toltec in Nahuatl means "mas-

ter craftsman." Something similar might have taken place in Egypt, Greece, India and China.

The cities built by the Sumerians though based on agriculture had a varied population. In addition to farmers and herdsmen there were fishermen, merchants, craftsmen, scribes, doctors, soldiers and priests. The Sumerian city has been the prototype of the cities that have dotted the planet for five thousand years. We of the present, writhing in the grip of an apparently insoluble urban crisis, may be witnessing the end of the second cycle of city building begun by the Sumerians.

3

Cities

and

Nature

I spent a good part of my life close to nature as migratory worker, lumberjack and placer miner. Mother Nature was breathing down my neck, so to speak, and I had the feeling that she did not want me around. I was bitten by every sort of insect, and scratched by burs, foxtails and thorns. My clothes were torn by buckbrush and tangled manzanita. Hard clods pushed against my ribs when I lay down to rest, and grime ate its way into every pore of my body. Everything around me was telling me all the time to roll up and be gone. I was an unwanted intruder. I could never be at home in nature the way trees, flowers and birds are at home in human habitations, even in the city. I did not feel at ease until my feet touched the paved road.

The road led to the city, and I knew with every fiber

of my being that the man-made world of the city was man's only home on this planet, his refuge from an inhospitable nonhuman cosmos.

Vaguely at first then more distinctly I realized that man is an eternal stranger on this planet. He became a stranger when he cut himself off from the rest of creation and became human. From this incurable strangeness stems our incurable insecurity, our unfulfillable craving for roots, our passion to cover the planet with man-made compounds, our need for the city—a citadel against the encroachment of nature.

I did not have to be a scholar to recognize that man's greatest achievements were conceived and realized not in the bracing atmosphere of plains, deserts, forests and mountaintops but in the crowded, noisy and smelly cities of ancient Mesopotamia and Egypt, and of Jerusalem, Athens, Florence, Amsterdam, Vienna, Paris, London and New York.

So true is it that the city is man's optimal creative milieu that even communion with the self is more attainable in the press and noise of the city than in the silence of the great outdoors. There is no genuine solitude outside the city.

2

There is in this country, particularly among the educated, a romantic, worshipful attitude toward nature. Nature is thought to be pure, innocent, serene, health-giving, the fountainhead of elevated thoughts and feelings. It is now a mark of intellectual distinction to run down man and extol nature. When some years ago I wrote an article in which I questioned nature's benevolence and suggested that the contest between man and nature has been the central drama of the universe I was rewarded with a shower of brickbats. A group of students in a San Diego high school, prompted no doubt by a nature-worshiping teacher, sent me insulting letters.

My hunch is that the attitude of the educated American toward nature is shaped and colored by European literature. Europe is one of the tamest parts of the world. Nowhere else are man and nature so much in each other's confidence. Imagine a subcontinent without a desert or a rampaging river, without hurricanes and tornadoes, and where you are never too far from a road or even an inn. Compare it with our savage continent. Open your newspaper any morning and you find reports of floods, tornadoes, hurricanes, hailstorms, sand-storms, pests and droughts. Sometimes when reading about nature's terrible visitations and its massacre of the innocents you wonder whether this continent is fit for human beings.

Fly over this country and you see what we have done. We have cast a net of concrete roads over a snarling continent and proceeded to tame each square. Every now and then there is a heaving and rumbling and the continent shakes us off its back.

On the Berkeley campus generations of young people, brainwashed by Wordsworth, Shelley, Tennyson and other poets of a manicured little island, have gone up to the woods to make love and come back swollen with poison oak. They have as yet not realized that on this continent woods and meadows are not what the poets say they are.

It is worth noting that Thoreau, who loved nature "because she is not man but a retreat from man," lived in a tame corner of America where the meadows were fertile, the hills gentle, and the woods hospitable.

The miracle is that we have taken a continent almost unfit for human beings and made it a cornucopia of plenty. The wilderness boys accuse us of ravaging and raping a continent. Actually, our mastery of nature is such that if we were so minded we could, in fifty years or so, regrow all the forests, replenish the soil, cleanse the rivers and the air of pollution, have buffalo herds again thundering on the plains, and make the continent as virgin as when we got here.

If this nation declines and decays it will be not because we have raped and ravaged a continent, but because we do not know how to build and maintain viable cities. America's destiny will be decided in the cities.

3

The attitude of the educated toward nature is particularly grotesque when you hear Latin American or African intellectuals enthuse about nature. Several years ago I had a visitor from Peru. He said he was a professor of sociology and also a novelist and poet. He was traveling as a guest of the State Department. I let him talk. It was unfortunate, he said, that this country was so far ahead technologically. The effort to catch up with us distorts and cripples other countries. He had all the clichés about the evils of our materialism, how it stifles and crushes the countries below the Rio Grande. I asked him how he liked San Francisco. He liked it fine, but he was disgusted with the Golden Gate Park. How dared we play tricks upon nature! The artificial lakes, creeks, mountains and waterfalls were a blasphemy. We lacked all reverence and made nature jump at our bidding.

First Things, Last Things

I said: "You come from a country where nature has repossessed all that the Incas built with infinite toil through the centuries. All the wonderful terraces, canals, roads, bridges and cities have become a wilderness. Nature is snatching the bread from your mouth. Your one and only problem is how to cope with nature, and your wildest dream should be a Peru turned into a Golden Gate Park. Yet you go on mouthing the inane clichés about nature that you picked up during your student days in Paris."

He stood up, a picture of outraged dignity. The Peruvian student from Berkeley who did the translating had a twinkle in his eyes, and we exchanged winks. Some time later I came upon a speech delivered by Fernando Belaunde Terry, then President of Peru, when he opened a network of rural roads. The last sentence of the speech read: "In Peru nature is the enemy."

As to Africa: We tend to forget that in Africa the battle that has to be won is not against colonialism but against nature. The chatter about Negritude and African identity and destiny is irrelevant to the central task, which is the conquest of African nature—primeval, relentless and aggressive—that enslaved and degraded man to an extent unknown anywhere else. The masters of Africa will be they—black or white—who know how to tame the forests, rivers and deserts, how to banish diseases and pests, and how to dispel the fear of nature embodied in brutalizing superstitions and rituals.

4

There are many who warn us that a cocky attitude toward nature spells trouble. Yet it is questionable whether a society awed by nature can be truly free. For freedom is basically freedom from nature, from the iron necessities and the implacable determinism which dominate nature. Moreover, a society awed by nature tends to equate power with nature, and would no more revolt against despotic power than it would against a natural calamity.

Equally vital is the fact that a society awed by nature is not likely to develop an effective technology for mastering nature. Man had to separate himself from nature, had to hole up in the city, a citadel against the encroachment of nature, before he could evolve a technology that liberated him from the animal imprisonment of nature with its wants, its menace and its bondage.* Only in the city could man become truly Promethean, in perpetual revolt against the iron laws which imprison all other forms of life.

* See Chapter 2.

Yet in Asia, where cities first made their appearance, the liberating role of the city has been shortlived. The outburst of discoveries and inventions in the earliest days of city building betokened a free, venturesome, questioning spirit. The people who were behind this onrush of achievements were more like us of the Occident than any in the intervening historic generations. The modern Occident picked up where the fabulous prehistoric craftsmen left off. But this self-reliant, venturesome spirit did not last. It was stifled by the total domination of kings, priests and scribes, and for millennia the cities of Asia stagnated in superstition and resignation. The civilizations of Asia functioned as if the answers were there before the questions.

In the Occident, self-governing cities have been for centuries nurseries of the human spirit, havens of welcome for strangers, stages of pageantry and high drama, the seedbed of freedom, art, literature, science and technology. But they have also been the abode of the devil, of the forces of corruption and dehumanization. In the Occident the city has been the greatest opportunity and the worst influence; a place of creation and decay, of freedom and subjection, of riches and poverty, of splendor and misery, of communion and lonesomeness—an optimal milieu for talent, character, vice and corruption.

For nature is both around and within us. Though the city has been the headquarters of the great movement of the human spirit to emancipate itself from the tyranny of matter, it has also been the place where man has been losing his battle with the nature that is sealed within him. The city has not freed man from the tyranny of his lusts, his savage impulses, his ferocious malice, and the dark destructive forces that lie in wait in the cellars of his psyche. If God is that which makes man human, and the devil that which dehumanizes him, then it is in the city and not in heaven that God and the devil are in perpetual combat.

5

Just now the devil is gaining the upper hand. In the past cities decayed because they lost the battle with nature around them and could no longer support themselves. Our cities are decaying at a moment when our victory over nature seems almost total, and affluence is widely diffused. The cores of our cities are packed with people who lack the enterprise to take advantage of opportunities, and the character to resist temptation. It is inside our cities just now that nature is striking back at us, pushing us back into the jungle, and turning us into primitive savages. For many Americans the city has become an environment as threatening as a neighboring tract of jungle is for an Indian or African villager. The

First Things, Last Things

words of Baltasar Gracián have never sounded more true than they do now: "The real wild beasts exist where most men live."

We are up against a predicament of the human condition: namely, the impossibility of coordinating the two fronts of man's battle with nature. Worse still, victory on one front is unavoidably followed by defeat on the other front. In our time the unprecedented triumphs of the technologist and the scientist have set the stage for the psychiatrist and the policeman. The moment we have gained mastery over things we are faced with the unsavory task of mastering men. Up to now in free societies, the mastery of men has been the automatic by-product of the effort to master things: social discipline has been a function of scarcity. Thus the present anarchy and terror in the cities make it questionable whether affluent societies can remain free.

The choice before us at present seems to be between two types of nonfree societies. (a) Our present society with its constitutional guarantees of individual freedom and its helplessness against willful individuals who mug, rob, rape, murder, bomb, riot and disrupt our institutions. It is clear that a society in the grip of fear is not free no matter how many the freedoms its constitution guarantees. (b) A dictatorship which deprives individuals of many freedoms but maintains order and security in the cities. There are already many people in this

[38]

country who would surrender many of their civil rights for a feeling of personal security.

Still, a dictatorship is not an acceptable solution of the apparent incompatibility between affluence and order. My hunch is that to keep stable and healthy a free affluent society must become a creative society. The destructive forces released by affluence must serve to fuel the creative process. There are indications that creativeness has its source in the tension between that which is most human and most unhuman in us. The historian Friedrich Meinecke was so impressed by the dark and impure origins of great cultural values that it seemed to him as though "God needed the devil to realize himself." Paul Valéry defines social peace as "the state of things in which the natural hostility of man toward man is manifested by creation instead of the destruction. . . . It is the period of creative competition and the struggle of inventions."

The sublimity of man manifests itself not in the purity and nobility of his impulses and motives but in the alchemy of his soul, which transmutes meanness and savagery into things of beauty and into thoughts and visions which reach unto heaven. The primordial slime is always within us and we become uniquely human as we process it.

We cope best with the devil not by fighting but by using him. Fighting the devil is at best a holding operation. A society preoccupied with the deliberate mastery of men is bound to lose much of its creative venturesomeness in both the material and spiritual spheres.

It remains to be seen whether it is possible to have a society free from want in which most people feel that they are growing, that they are realizing capacities and mastering skills, and have neither the time nor the inclination to do harm to their fellow men. My guess is that the unit of a creative society will be not a county or a parish but a school district. The country will be divided into thousands of school districts, each responsible for the realization of the natural and human resources within a relatively small area. The unfolding of human capacities requires a social unit in which people of different pursuits, interests, skills and tastes know each other, commune daily with each other, emulate, antagonize and spur each other. It is likely that such a social unit may also be optimal for the solution of the problems of race relations, crime, chronic poverty, drugs etc. which at this moment seem almost insoluble.

4

The Tilt
of the Social
Landscape

There is probably no better way of gauging the nature of a society than by finding the direction in which ambition and talent flow. In what fields are there to be found the greatest rewards? What achievements does a society prize most?

In this country until not very long ago the social landscape was steeply tilted toward the marketplace. Most energies and talents flowed toward business. The American businessman, served by lawyers and politicians, ruled the roost. He dominated not only the marketplace but "society," the newspapers, the universities, and his influence made itself felt in all branches of government. His foundations subsidized the unprecedented advance in science and learning, and his venturesome spirit fueled new technological breakthroughs.

First Things, Last Things

In the early years of this century the Englishman G. Lowes Dickinson remarked that "In America business holds the place in popular esteem that is held by arms in Germany, by letters in France, and by Public Life in England."

American businessmen have often struck foreign observers as a species apart, unlike businessmen elsewhere. "The American merchant," wrote Professor Hugo Münsterberg, "works for money in exactly the sense that a great painter works for money; the high price which is paid for his picture is a very welcome indication of the general appreciation of his art." In Europe "the merchant does not feel himself to be a free creator like the artist and scholar." Another foreign observer saw the American businessman as classless—"grandee, entrepreneur, and proletarian all in one." To the Indian writer Nirad Chadhuri the American businessman is "the old European conquistador in a new incarnation."

There was a time in this country when the children of scholars, writers and artists felt underprivileged that their fathers were not businessmen. In *Notes of a Son and a Brother* Henry James tells how he and his brother William were mortified that their father was a scholar and writer rather than a businessman.

To me the grandiose self-assurance of the American businessman is exemplified in the San Francisco merchant Adolph Sutro who proposed during the Civil

War that Lincoln should contract out the taking of Richmond to a businessman who would deliver it on time.

2

The unchallenged paramountcy of the American businessman had its start in the middle of the last century. The first half of the nineteenth century was the golden age of the gentry, of Emerson's gentlemen, whose hallmarks were breeding, education, cultural interest and public service. But the opening of the West in the middle of the century caught the imagination of the young. The sons of the gentry scattered in all directions. Many who might have become scholars, divines, writers and artists were seeking their fortunes in railroads, mining, oil wells and all sorts of business undertakings. The social landscape tilted sharply toward the marketplace.

One of the significant consequences of a sharp tilt of the social landscape is an increase in misplacement. In this country, for over a century, many who were meant for other things were washed into business careers. Paradoxically, these misplaced persons acted as energizers and innovators and impressed their style on a sphere of activity to which they did not really belong. It was not conventional businessmen but misplaced poets and philosophers who gave American business its Promethean sweep and drive. To a potential philosopher turned businessman all action is of one kind, and he combines steel mills, mines, factories and so on the way a philosopher collates and generalizes ideas. Clearly the foreign observers quoted above were not imagining things when they sensed the unconventional nature of American businessmen.

Misplacement induces a tendency toward overstepping, initiating and innovating, and it would be difficult to exaggerate the role played by misplaced persons in shaping the attitudes of a class or even of a whole society. In France where the social landscape is tilted toward letters and the arts, the chances are that potential business tycoons will find themselves trapped in the career of intellectuals; and it is these misplaced businessmen who are giving French intellectual life its passionate activism, and are probably responsible for the ceaseless innovating in French literature and art. To a potential businessman turned intellectual words and ideas are not an end in themselves but a preliminary to action, and he sees commitment and history making as vital components of an intellectual existence. He is also likely to equate change with growth. Often when face to face with outstanding French intellectuals one has the feeling that in America men of their character and caliber would occupy high positions in business and industry.

The Tilt of the Social Landscape

It is perhaps true that cultural, social and political innovations are usually the work of potential men of action trapped in the career of men of words, while grand innovations in commerce and industry are likely to be the work of potential philosophers cast in the role of businessmen.

3

There are as yet no signs of a diminution in the initiative and drive of American business. More than ever, American business is the envy of, and a model for, much of the world. What Stalin said of American business in the 1920s holds true today: "It is that indomitable force which knows and recognizes no obstacle, which by its businesslike perseverance washes away all and every obstacle."

Nevertheless, inside America, the prestige of the businessman is no longer what it used to be. The Great Depression knocked him off his pedestal, and despite his prodigious achievements since then he has not climbed back to a position of unquestioned paramountcy. Moreover, since Sputnik, other walks of life are vying with business in their appeal to the ambitious and the talented.

It is difficult to recapture now how crushed the United States was by Khrushchev's Sputnik toy. We reacted hysterically. We set out to produce scientists and technicians wholesale, and diverted a flood of billions into the universities. Energies and talents flowed in the wake of the billions. Thus a toy, a mere gimmick, brought about a change in the tilt of our social landscape.

The life of an outstanding professor is nowadays more attractive and prestigious than the life of a successful businessman. A scientist in particular, if he is any good at all, has prospects of adventure and renown undreamt-of by business tycoons. Nor are the material rewards to be sneezed at. There are all sorts of scholarships, fellowships, grants from government and foundations, fabulous fees from corporations, and national and international prizes.

Unlike the James brothers, the young nowadays are likely to be proud of a father who is a scholar or an author rather than a businessman. Nor is it at all certain at present that a beautiful woman who could have her pick of husbands would choose a rich businessman rather than a promising scientist or artist.

Instead of potential philosophers and poets being washed into business careers the likelihood is now of potential wheelers and dealers pawing their way up academic ladders, and throwing their weight around in literary and artistic cliques. Personal misplacement and the resulting tendency toward overstepping and innovating are more visible at present on the campus than in the marketplace. The people who make all the noise on the campus and in the literary-intellectual salons of Manhattan and San Francisco are basically men of action cast in the role of men of words. Many of them would be truly at home wheeling and dealing on Wall Street, buying and selling factories, building sparkling new towns in the desert, and doing heaven knows what else. Their cries for relevance in the universities and for drastic social and political reforms echo the needs and the hungers of brilliant organizers and manipulators separated from their natural métier. The trouble is not chiefly that our universities are unfit for students but that many present-day students are unfit for universities. The resemblance to the French pattern is patent, and the vague feeling that the educated segment of the American population is becoming un-American is not based on illusion.

4

It is of interest that in the Jewish segment of the population the diversion of energies from the marketplace to the academy preceded by several decades the present change in the tilt of the social landscape. In Jewish families it has long been more likely for the son of a businessman to become a professor than the other way around.

It has always seemed noteworthy to me that with their unquestioned talent for business the Jews have not figured as outstanding innovators in commerce and industry. There has been no Jewish Ford, Morgan, Carnegie or Rockefeller. On the other hand, Jewish activities in the cultural sphere show markedly the tendency toward overstepping and innovating connected with personal misplacement. The popular identification of Jews with business does not echo a significant truth. Actually, the Jews' activity in the cultural sphere is far more vital to a society than their performance in the marketplace. Germany offers an instructive illustration of this truth. The miraculous economic recovery of Western Germany after the Second World War proceeded wholly without Jewish participation, whereas in the realm of the spirit the absence of the Jewish element is keenly felt by concerned Germans. "A modern literature," says a contemporary German critic, "is un-thinkable without the voice of Israel." Marcel Reich-Ranicki, a Polish Jew who fled from Communist Poland to West Germany in 1958, is now one of the most vital voices in German literature.

No one will question the excellence of Jews as men of action—not only in the marketplace but on the battlefield and in politics. But their vitalizing and in-

novating faculties come to the surface when their energies and talents are diverted into cultural channels. The
Jewish equivalents of industrial empire builders and of
political colossi are found in philosophy and the sci-
ences. Marx, Freud and Einstein have shaped the temper
of our time. It is a paradox that the twentieth century
which saw the fearful slaughter of Jews should be, to a
considerable extent, a Jewish century.

5

As pointed out, American business is still riding high.
Though we are told that talented young Americans tend
to avoid careers involved in any way with production
and economic affairs, business still manages, with some
extra wooing, to recruit talented and enterprising members of the new generation. Nevertheless, there are indications that the future crop of business leaders will
markedly deviate from the type that has dominated
American business for over a century. The ease with
which business has been adjusting itself to the tastes and
styles of the young is breathtaking, and betokens an
incredible flexibility. Think of house organs of businesses
like *Time* and *Life* magazines assuming a psychedelic
tint overnight! It seems, therefore, not improbable that
a decade from now we may see long-haired business

tycoons bedecked with beads and medallions, at home in literary-intellectual salons, and oriented toward public service. Though there is no reason to assume that the new businessmen will not maintain an undiminished drive toward expansion, innovation and fabulous profits, they will yet help create a new style of life and a new social climate. The remarkable thing is that the new style will have much in it reminiscent of the pre-industrial era—of the age of the gentry. The 1980s will have much in them to remind us of the 1840s.

The present-day young who enter business are impatient of apprenticeship; they feel themselves born professionals. The strange thing is that the middle-aged bosses, in both business and politics, seem eager to recognize "the tremendous resource and store of energy in this generation." It is likely, therefore, that the near future will see many young faces in leading positions in business and politics. This would reinforce the impression of a return to the past. For the ascendancy of the middle-aged is a relatively recent phenomenon. Through most of the past the young had their hands on the reins of power, and played leading roles in both war and peace.

It is of course conceivable that a rapid radicalization of the universities might disrupt the liaison between business and the educated segment of the population. Should this happen, one ought to expect American business to establish its own technical schools and institutes, in which pure and applied science, the humanities, and practical paid work would be so intermixed as to obviate the emergence of the highbrow, militant posture of the alienated academic. Such a development would diminish the resources and prestige of established universities, and might, to some extent, reverse the trend started by Sputnik.

5

The Young
and
the Middle-Aged

The conspicuous role played by the young in our society at present has prompted a widely held assumption that the young constitute a higher percentage of the population than they did in the past. Actually, in this country, the percentage of the under-twenty-five age group has remained fairly constant through several decades—it hovers around forty-seven percent. The high school and college age group—fourteen to twenty-four—has remained close to fifteen percent. The nation as a whole has not been getting younger. The median age of all Americans in 1910 was twenty-four. Today it is twenty-seven; and it is likely to go up since the birth rate right now is very low.

The conspicuousness of the young is due to their greater visibility and audibility. They have become more flamboyant, more demanding, more violent, more knowledgeable, and more experienced. The general impression is that nowadays the young act like the spoiled children of the rich. We are discovering that there is such a thing as an "ordeal of affluence," that diffused affluence subjects the social order to greater strain and threatens social stability more than does diffused poverty. Order and discipline have up to now been attributes generated in the battle against want. Society itself originated in the vital need for a joint effort to wrest a livelihood from grudging nature. Not only our material but our moral and spiritual values are predicated on the immemorial curse: "In the sweat of thy face shalt thou eat bread." Thus diffused affluence unavoidably creates a climate of disintegrating values with its fallout of anarchy.

In the past, breakdowns of value affected mainly the older segment of the population. This was true of the breakdown of the Graeco-Roman civilization, of the crisis which gave birth to the Reformation, and of the periods of social disintegration which preceded the French, the Russian and the Nazi revolutions. That our present crisis particularly affects the young is due partly to the fact that widespread affluence is robbing a modern society of whatever it has left of puberty rites to routinize the attainment of manhood. Never before has the passage from boyhood to manhood been so difficult and

explosive. The children both of the well-to-do and of
families on welfare are prevented from having a share in
the world's work and of proving their manhood by doing a man's work and getting a man's pay. Crime in the
streets and insolence on the campus are sick forms of
adolescent self-assertion. The young account for an
ever-increasing percentage of crimes against persons
and property. The peak years for crimes of violence
are eighteen to twenty, followed by the twenty-one-to-
twenty-four age group.

Even under ideal conditions the integration of the
young into the adult world is beset with strains and
difficulties. We feel ill at ease when we have to adjust
ourselves to fit in. The impulse is to change the world
to fit us rather than the other way around. Only where
there are, as in primitive societies, long-established rites
of passage, or where the opportunities for individual
self-assertion are fabulous, does growing up proceed
without excessive growing pains.

Can a modern affluent society institute some form of
puberty rites to ease the passage from boyhood to manhood? It is of interest in this connection that among the
Bantu tribes in South Africa work is replacing the ritual
related to puberty. It used to be that a young man had
to kill a lion or an enemy to prove his manhood. Today
many young natives do not feel they have become full-
fledged adults until they have put in a stint in the mines.

First Things, Last Things

Could not a ritual of work be introduced in this country? Every boy and girl on reaching seventeen, or on graduating from high school, would be given an opportunity to spend two years earning a living at good pay. There is an enormous backlog of work to be done both inside and outside the cities. Federal, state and city governments and also business and labor would pool their resources to supply the necessary jobs and training.

The routinization of the passage from boyhood to manhood would contribute to the solution of many of our pressing problems. I cannot think of any other undertaking that would dovetail so many of our present difficulties into opportunities for growth.

Though the percentage of the young, as pointed out, has remained constant through several decades, there has been a spectacular increase in the percentage of adolescents. At present adolescence comprises a wider age range than it did in the past. Affluence is keeping persons in their late twenties in a state of delayed manhood, while television has lowered the threshold of adolescence. Nowadays, ten-year-olds have the style of life and the bearing of adolescents. Even children under ten have an astounding familiarity with the intricacies and the mechanics of the adult world. By the time children enter kindergarten they have spent more hours learning about their world from television than they will spend later in classrooms earning a college degree. It is a paradox that at a time when youths rioting in Chicago are called "mere kids," there are actually few genuine kids any more.

The contemporary blurring of childhood is not unprecedented. During the Middle Ages children were viewed and treated as miniature adults. Nothing in medieval dress distinguished the child from the adult. The moment children could walk and talk they entered the adult world, and took part in the world's work. In subsequent centuries the concept of childhood became more clearly defined. Yet even as late as 1835 schoolbooks in this country made no concession to childhood in vocabulary or sophistication. Child labor so widely practiced in the first half of the nineteenth century, and which we find abhorrent, was not totally anomalous in a society that did not have a vivid view of childhood as a sheltered, privileged age.

To counteract an old man's tendency to snort at the self-important young, I keep reminding myself that until the middle of the nineteenth century the young acted effectively as members of political parties, creators of business enterprises, advocates of new philosophical doctrines, and leaders of armies. Most of the wars which figure in our history books were fought by teenagers. There were fourteen-year-old lieutenants in Louis XIV's army. In one of his armies the oldest soldier was under eighteen. The middle-aged came to the fore with the

industrial revolution. The experience and capital necessary to make an industrialist required a long apprenticeship. One might say that from the middle of the nineteenth to the middle of the twentieth century the world
was run by and for the middle-aged. The post-industrial
age seems to be groping its way back to an immemorial
situation interrupted by the industrial revolution.

2

I said that the middle-aged came to the fore with the
industrial revolution. Another way of putting it is that
the middle-aged came into their own with the full entrance of the middle class onto the stage of history. The
present discomfiture of the middle-aged is a symptom of
a downturn in the fortunes of the middle class.

Adolescence as a clearly marked phase in the life of
the individual, and the practice of keeping physically
mature males in a state of delayed manhood, are middle-
class phenomena. The young of the working class and
of the aristocracy come early in touch with the realities
of life, and are not kept waiting in the wings. In neither
the working class nor the aristocracy does age have the
vital meaning it has in the middle class.

Industrialization was the creation of the middle class.
It is questionable whether the spectacular "mastery of

things," the taming of nature on a global scale, could have been achieved by other human types. No other ruling class succeeded so well in energizing the masses, and infusing them with an automatic readiness to work. Aristocrats and intellectuals know how to generate in a population a readiness to fight and die, but they cannot induce an uncoerced, whole-hearted participation of the masses in the world's work.

Indeed, it is doubtful whether a non-middle-class society can be modern. Domination by aristocrats, intellectuals, workers or soldiers results in a return to the past—to feudalism, the Middle Ages, or even the ancient river-valley civilizations. It is not as yet certain whether it is possible to have a free-wheeling science, literature and art, or even a genuine machine age without a middle class.

Yet, despite its unprecedented achievements, the middle class is just now on the defensive, unsure of its footing. With the consummation of the industrial revolution and the approach of affluence the middle class seems to have nowhere to go. It no longer feels itself in possession of the true and only view possible for sensible people. One begins to wonder whether the unglamorous, hard-working middle class, so essential to the process of production in a climate of scarcity, is becoming anachronistic in an age of plenty where distribution is the chief problem. Middle-class society is being strained to the breaking point not, as Marx predicted, by ever-increasing misery but by ever-increasing affluence. The coming of affluence has found the middle class unequipped and unprepared for a return to Eden.

Early in the nineteenth century Saint-Simon characterized the coming of the industrial age as the passage "from the management of men to the administration of things." He did not foresee that once the industrial revolution had run its course there would have to come a reversion from the administration of things to the management of men. Up to quite recently the middle class did not have to bother overmuch with the management of men since scarcity (unfulfilled needs), the factory, long working hours, etc. tamed and disciplined people automatically. Now with affluence and leisure people are no longer kept in line by circumstances. Discipline has to be implanted and order enforced from without. It is at this point that "men of words" and charismatic leaders—people who deal with magic—come into their own. The middle class, lacking magic, is bungling the job.

3

Thus as the post-industrial age unfolds we begin to suspect that what is waiting for us around the corner is not a novel future but an immemorial past. It begins to look as if the fabulous century of the middle class and the middle-aged has been a detour, a wild loop that turns upon itself, and ends where it began. We are returning to the rutted highway of history which we left a hundred years ago in a mad rush to tame a savage continent and turn it into a cornucopia of plenty. We see all around us the lineaments of a pre-industrial pattern emerging in the post-industrial age. We are rejoining the ancient caravan, a caravan dominated by the myths and magic of elites, and powered by the young.

In this country the coming of the post-industrial age may mean the loss of all that made America new—the only new thing in the world. America will no longer be the common man's continent. The common people of Europe eloped with history to America and have lived in common-law marriage with it, unhallowed by the incantations of men of words. But the elites are finally catching up with us. We can hear the swish of leather as saddles are heaved on our backs. The intellectuals and the young, booted and spurred, feel themselves born to ride us.

The phenomenal increase of the student population is shaping the attitudes and aspirations of the young. There are now more students in America than farmers. For the first time in America there is a chance that alienated intellectuals, who see our way of life as an instrument of debasement and dehumanization, might shape a new generation in their own image. The young's sympathy for the Negro and the poor goes hand in hand with an elitist conceit that pits them against the egalitarian masses. They will fight for the Negro and the poor but they have no use for common folk who work and moonlight to take care of their own. They see a free-wheeling democracy as a society stupefied by "the narcotic of mass culture." They reserve their wrath for the institutions in which common people are most represented: unions, Congress, the police, and the army. Professor Edgar Z. Friedenberg thinks that "elitism is the great and distinctive contribution students are making to American society." Democracy is for the dropouts; for the elites an aristocratic brotherhood.

Yet one cannot help wonder how inevitable the future is that seemingly is waiting for us around the corner. Might not the common people, so cowed and silent at this moment, eventually kick up their heels, and trample would-be elitists in the dirt? There is no earthly reason why the common people who for over a century have been doing here things which in other countries are reserved for elites, should not be capable of overcoming the present crisis.

The militant young are not as formidable as they seem. Many of them, stoned and decked out in peacock finery, are on the way to the ashcan. A paean to the young sounds hollow when you watch their goings-on in cities and on campuses. Should America come into the keeping of militant youth—white and black—we would have a vast Haiti, totally integrated, totally chaotic and stagnant, and lorded by a Doc Duvalier and the Tontons Macoutes.

6

Whose Country?

Nowhere at present is there such a measureless loathing of their country by educated people as in America. An excellent historian thinks Americans are "the most frightening people in the world," and a foremost philologist sees America as "the most aggressive power in the world, the greatest threat to peace and to international cooperation." Others call America a "pig heaven," "a monster with 200 million heads," "a cancer on the body of mankind."

Novelists, playwrights, poets, essayists and philosophers depict America as the land of the dead. It is a country where sensitive souls are starved and flayed, where nothing nourishes and everything hurts. Nowhere, they say, is there such a boring monotony: monotony of talk, monotony of ideas, monotony of aim, and monotony of outlook on the world. One American writer says, "America is no place for an artist. A corn-fed hog enjoys a better life than a creative artist." One she intellectual maintains that "the quality of American life is an insult to the possibilities of human growth."

It is hard to believe that this savage revulsion derives from specific experiences with persons and places. What is there in America that prevents an educated person from shaping his life, from making the most of his in-born endowments? With all its faults and blemishes, this country gives a man elbow room to do what is nearest to his heart. It is incredible how easy it is here to cut oneself off from vulgarity, conformity, specious-ness and other corrupting influences and infections. For those who want to be left alone to realize their capacities and talents, this is an ideal country.

The trouble is, of course, that the alienated intellectual does not want to be left alone. He wants to be listened to and be taken seriously. He wants to influence affairs, have a hand in making history, and feel important. He is free to speak and write as he pleases, and can probably make himself heard and read more easily than one who would defend America. But he can neither sway elections nor shape policy. Even when his excellence as a writer, artist, scholar, scientist or educator is generally recognized and rewarded he does not feel himself part of the power structure. In no other country has there been so little liaison between men of words and the men of action who exercise power. The body of intellectuals in America has never been integrated with and congenial to the politicians and businessmen who make things happen. Indeed, the uniqueness of modern America derives in no small part from the fact that America has kept intellectuals away from power and paid little attention to their political views.

The 1960s have made it patent that much of the intellectual's dissent is fueled by a hunger for power. The appearance of potent allies—militant blacks and students —has emboldened the intellectual to come out into the open. He still feels homeless in America, but the spectacle of proud authority, in cities and on campuses, always surrendering before threats of violence is to him a clear indication that middle-class society is about to fall apart, and he is all set to pick up the pieces.

There is no doubt that in our permissive society the intellectual has far more liberty than he can use; and the more his liberty and the less his capacity to make use of it, the louder his clamor for power—power to deprive other people of liberty.

First Things, Last Things

2

The intellectual's allergy to America shows itself with particular clarity in what has happened to many foreign intellectuals who found asylum here during the Hitler decade. It is legitimate to assume that they had no anti-American preconceptions when they arrived. They were on the contrary predisposed to see what was best in their host country. Though no one has recorded what Herbert Marcuse said when he landed in New York in 1934 it is safe to assume that he did not see Americans as one-dimensional men, and did not equate our tolerance with oppression, our freedom with slavery, and our good nature with simple-mindedness. We have a record of what some other foreign intellectuals said when they arrived in the 1930s. It is worth quoting in full the words of Olga Schnitzler, the widow of Arthur Schnitzler: "So much is here to learn and to see. Everyone has been given an opportunity. Everyone who has not been completely worn out experiences here a kind of rebirth. Everyone feels what a grandiose, complex and broad-minded country America is, how well and free one can live among these people without perfidy and malice. Yes, we have lost a homeland but we have found a world."

[74]

Once they have settled down and found their place many of these intellectuals began to feel constrained and stifled by the forwardness and the mores of the plebeian masses. They missed the aristocratic climate of the old world. Inevitably too, they became disdainful of our lowbrow, practical intelligence. They began to doubt whether Americans had the high-caliber intelligence to solve the problems of a complex, difficult age. Hardly one of them bethought himself that in Europe, when intellectuals of their kind had a hand in shaping and managing affairs, things had not gone too well. There is something that prevents them from sensing the unprecedented nature of the American experiment: that the rejected of Europe have come here together, tamed a savage continent in an incredibly short time and, unguided by intellectuals, fashioned the finest society on a large scale the world has so far seen.

Scratch an intellectual and you find a would-be aristocrat who loathes the sight, the sound and the smell of common folk. Professor Marcuse has lived among us for over thirty years and now, in old age, his disenchantment with this country is spilling over into book after book. He is offended by the intrusion of the vulgar, by the failure of egalitarian America to keep common people in their place. He is frightened by "the degree to which the population is allowed to break the peace where there is still peace and silence, to be ugly and uglify things, to ooze familiarity and to offend against good form." The vulgar invade "the small reserved sphere of existence" and compel exquisite Marcusian souls to partake of their sounds, sights and smells.

To a shabby would-be aristocrat like Professor Marcuse there is something fundamentally wrong with a society in which the master and the worker, the typist and the boss's daughter do not live totally disparate lives. Everything good in America seems to him a sham and a fraud.

3

An interesting peculiarity of present-day dissenting intellectuals is their lack of animus toward the rich. They are against the government, the Congress, the army and the police, and against corporations and unions, but hardly anything is being said or written against "the money changers in the temple," "the economic royalists," "the malefactors of great wealth" and "the maniacs wild for gold" who were the butts of vituperation in the past. Indeed, there is nowadays a certain rapport between the rich and the would-be revolutionaries. The outlandish role the rich are playing in the affluent society is one of the surprises of our time.

Whose Country?

Though the logic of it seems now fairly evident, I doubt whether anyone had foreseen that affluence would radicalize the upper rich and the lowest poor and nudge them toward an alliance against those in the middle. Whatever we have of revolution just now is financed largely by the rich.

In order to feel rich you have to have poor people around you. In an affluent society riches lose their uniqueness—people no longer find fulfillment in being rich. And when the rich cannot feel rich they begin to have misgivings about success—not enough to give up the fruits of success, but enough to feel guilty about it and emote soulfully about the grievances of the disadvantaged, and the sins of the status quo. It seems that every time a millionaire opens his mouth nowadays he confesses the sins of our society in public. Now it so happens that the rich do indeed have a lot to feel guilty about. They live in exclusive neighborhoods, send their children to private schools, and use every loophole to avoid paying taxes. But what they confess in public are not their private sins but the sins of society, the sins of the rest of us, and it is our breasts they are beating into a pulp. They feel guilty and ashamed, they say, because the mass of people, who do most of the work and pay much of the taxes, are against integrated schools and housing, and do not tax themselves to the utmost to fight

the evils which beset our cities. We are discovering that
in an affluent society the rich have a monopoly on
righteousness.

Moreover, the radicalized rich have radical children.
There is no generation gap here. The most violent
cliques of the New Left are made up of the children of
the rich. The Weathermen, to whom workingmen are
"honky bastards," have not a member with a working-
man's background. The behavior of the extremist young
makes sense when seen as the behavior of spoiled brats
used to instant fulfillment who expect the solutions to
life's problems to be there on demand. And just as in
former days aristocratic sprigs horsewhipped peasants,
so at present the children of the rich are riding rough-
shod over community sensibilities.* The rich parents
applaud and subsidize their revolutionary children, and
probably brag about them at dinner parties.

As I said, the alienated rich are one of the surprises
of our time. It is not surprising to be told that America
is a country where intellectuals are least at home. But it
is startling to realize that the rich are not, and probably

* "It does seem to me that the young consider themselves an elite,
more deserving of life and privileges than anybody else. The French
aristocracy of the 18th century had rights like that: they were able to
express themselves say sexually or in other ways that the bourgeoisie
was not. The bourgeoisie were a restrained class . . . but the nobility
was free to dress up—which is what the young now do—to do as they
liked, relieve themselves in public places and so on." Saul Bellow in the
Jerusalem Post Weekly, July 13, 1970.

never have been, wholly at ease in this country. The fact that it is easy to get rich in America has not made it a rich man's country. The rich have always had it better elsewhere—better service, more deference and more leisure and fun. In America the rich have not known how to savor their riches, and many of them have not known how to behave and have come to a bad end.

4

There is a story about a British intellectual who traveled through this country toward the end of the last century. He was appalled by the monotony and unimaginativeness of the names of the towns he saw through the train window: Thomasville, Richardsville, Harrysville, Marysville and so on. He had not an inkling of the import of what he was seeing: namely, that for the first time in history common people—any Tom, Dick and Harry—could build a town and name it after his own or his wife's name. At one station an old Irishwoman got on the train and sat next to him. When she heard his muttering and hissing she said: "This is a blessed country, Sir. I think God made it for the poor." De Crèvecoeur, in the eighteenth century, saw America as an asylum where "the poor of Europe have by some means met together." The poor everywhere have looked on America as their Eldorado. They voted for it with their legs by coming over in their millions.

Yet during the 1960s poverty became one of the chief problems which plague this country; one of several nagging problems—like race relations, violence, drugs, inflation—which defy solution. From being a land of opportunity for the poor America has become a dead-end street for some fifteen million unemployables, 80 percent of them white, and most of them trapped in the cores of big cities. Money, better housing and special schooling have little effect. Our society is showing itself unduly awkward in the attempt to turn the chronically poor into productive, useful citizens. Whereas in the not too distant past it was axiomatic that society lived at the expense of the poor, the present-day poor, like the Roman proletariat, live at the expense of society.

We have been transformed by affluence to a psychological age. Impersonal factors, including money, no longer play a decisive role in human affairs. It seems that by mastering things we have drained things of their potency to shape men's lives. It is remarkable that common people are aware of this fact. They know that at present money cannot cure crime, poverty, etc., whereas the social doctors go on prescribing an injection of so many billions for every social ailment.

In Chapter 2, "The Birth of Cities," it has been suggested that in the earliest cities suburbs made their appearance as a refuge for dropouts who could not make the grade in the city. When eventually the cities decayed the suburbs continued as the earliest villages. In our cities the process has been reversed. The dropouts are stagnating in the cores of the cities, while people who are ideally suited for city life seek refuge in the suburbs. The indications are that we shall not have viable cities until we lure the chronically poor out of the cities and induce the exiled urbanites to return.

The diffusion of affluence has accelerated the absorption of the majority of workingmen into the middle class. The unemployable poor, left behind, feel isolated and exposed, and it is becoming evident that a middle-class society which hugs the conviction that everyone can take care of himself is singularly inept in helping those who cannot help themselves. If the rich cannot feel rich in an affluent society, the poor have never felt poorer.

The chronically poor have to be reconstructed, and the process of human renewal partakes of magic. A medicine man like Castro, who is a stumbling block to people who know how to help themselves and want to be left alone, has been doing wonders with the chronically poor. It is becoming doubtful whether the problem of chronic poverty can be solved in a typical American milieu.

First Things, Last Things

In a highly original essay, "Strategic Hamlets in America," Professor David Pender of the University of South Carolina outlines a plan for resettling the chronically poor in cooperative hamlets on the periphery of the big cities. He feels that "although the chronically poor have been on our shores for generations, most of them have never been integrated with the main body of American life and might as well be treated as if they 'just got off the boat.' " The purpose of the hamlets is to bring about "a change in the habits, attitudes and way of looking at the world of a group who, to some degree, have become psychological cripples." The human reconstruction and renewal of the poor will have to take place in a non-American environment. What the poor need is "the cohesive spirit akin to that of a Scottish clan or an African tribe or an Israeli Kibbutz."

In short, the present-day poor, like the intellectuals and the rich, do not feel wholly at home in America.

5

Whose country, then, is America? It is the country of the common, the common men and women, a good 70 percent of the population, who do most of the work, pay much of the taxes, crave neither power nor importance, and want to be left alone to live pleasurable humdrum lives. "The founders of the United States," said Lord Charnwood, "did deliberately aspire to found a commonwealth in which common men and women should count for more than elsewhere."

Again and again you come up against the mystery of what happens to common folk when they land on our shores. It is like a homecoming. They find here their natural habitat, their ideal milieu, which brings their energies and capacities into full play.

Tasks which in other countries are reserved for a select minority, for a specially trained elite, are in this country performed by every Tom, Dick and Harry. Not only did common Americans build and name towns, but they also founded states, propagated new faiths, commanded armies, wrote books and ran for the highest offices. It is this that makes America unprecedentedly new.

It tickled me no end that the astronauts who landed on the moon were not elite-conscious intellectuals but lowbrow ordinary Americans.* It has been the genius of common Americans to achieve the momentous in an unmomentous matter-of-fact way. If space exploration remains in their keeping they will soon make of it an

---

* Professor Victor C. Ferkiss, author of *Technological Man*, sees the astronauts as "thoroughly conventional and middle-class and essentially dull people who would make such nice neighbors and such unlikely friends." Could these, he wonders, "be the supermen whom the race had struggled for a million years to produce?"

everyday routine accessible to all. The intellectuals call this giving access to the vulgar—vulgarization. The intellectual's inclination is to complicate things, to make them so abstruse and difficult that they are accessible only to the initiated few. Where the intellectuals are in power, prosaic tasks become Promethean undertakings. I have yet to meet an intellectual who truly believes that common people can govern themselves and run things without outstanding leaders. In the longshoremen's union the intellectuals have a nervous breakdown any time a common, barely literate longshoreman runs for office and gets elected.

To me it seems axiomatic that the common people everywhere are our natural allies, and that our chief contribution to the advancement of mankind should be the energizing and activation of common folk. We must learn how to impart to common people everywhere the technological, political and social skills which would enable them to dispense with the tutorship of the upper classes and the intellectuals. We must deflate the pretensions of self-appointed elites. These elites will hate us no matter what we do, and it is legitimate for us to help dump them into the dustbin of history.

Our foreign aid to backward countries in Asia, Africa and Latin America should be tailored to the needs of common people rather than of the elites. The elites hanker for the trappings of the twentieth century. They want steel mills, airlines, skyscrapers, etc. Let them get these trappings from elitist Russia. Our gift to the people in backward countries should be the capacity for self-help. We must show them how to get bread, human dignity and strength by their own efforts. We must know how to stiffen their backbone so that they will insist on getting their full share of the good life and not allow themselves to be sacrificed to the Moloch of a mythical future.

There is an America hidden in the soil of every country and in the soul of every people. It is our task to help common people everywhere discover their America at home.

7

The Spirit
of
an Age

Up to the end of the eighteenth century there was nowhere a vivid awareness of epochs and ages totally distinct from, and almost incomprehensible to, each other. Even in this country up to 1800 the quality of everyday life was not totally different from what it was, say, four thousand years ago in Mesopotamia and Egypt. Despite a succession of momentous historical events, of empires rising and falling, of new religions, conceptions, discoveries and inventions, the first forty centuries or so of recorded history, even if not, in the words of Ibn Khaldoon, "as alike as drops of water," had enough in common to make the idea of the spirit of an age meaningless. George Washington would have felt at home in Cheops's Egypt. Even Napoleon could have engaged in profitable discourse with any of the

Pharaohs, though if he had met a modern American President they would have had little to say to each other.

The feeling that the present is so novel and unprecedented that, living in it, one can only by an effort of the imagination understand the past came with the industrial revolution. Around 1850 the Occident was catapulted into a trajectory away from the ageless, rutted highway of history.

Does this mean that drastic differences in technology make ages incomprehensible to each other? Is the spirit of an age an emanation of technology?

The eloquent Africanist Laurens Van Der Post in his travels through Russia in 1963 was struck by the similarity between the patient, submissive humanity he saw in Russia and the primitive black crowds he had seen in African railroad stations and public offices. He saw "the same silent acceptance of their fate implicit in the expression and attitude of these waiting figures." Everywhere he went the thought came to him unbidden that "for all its twentieth century trappings, its applied science, its protestation of being objective and rational, Russia was basically neither new nor modern but is a reversion to an exceedingly ancient and primitive state of spirit." He began to suspect that one could not have a real understanding of Russian behavior unless one saw in it an expression of "an archaic, religious and profoundly superstitious system."

Clearly, the technology of present-day Russia, not dissimilar from, and not too far behind, the technology of America, has not made of Russia a nation of our time, imbued with the spirit of our age.

2

Why has an advanced technology not made Russia a modern country?

Saint-Simon, as we have seen, characterized the coming of the industrial age as a passage from the management of men to the administration of things. Now, there is no doubt that in Russia the Communist party has poured enormous wealth and energies into "the administration of things," and its feats in mastering nature are among the outstanding achievements of the twentieth century. But it is also true that in Russia the central preoccupation has been and still is the management of men—the regimentation of people in every sphere of life. To a ruling Communist party, its role as initiator and director of activities in every field is more vital than the spontaneous flow of copious energies which is the hallmark of a modern society. The advanced technology which to some extent liberates the Russian people from the animal imprisonment of nature cannot liberate them from the menagerie instituted by an orthodox Communist party. The Russian people face the absolute power of the Communist apparatus with the same fatalistic submissiveness and superstitious dread with which primitive humanity faces the inexorable and inscrutable powers of nature.

One of the startling discoveries of our time is that revolutions are not revolutionary. We have been slow to realize that revolutions lead not to a wholly new future but back to a distant past. The most revolutionary changes during the last several decades have occurred in nonrevolutionary countries. Think of what has happened in this country: in less than two decades we have been transported into a new age. Nineteen fifty seems far off and semi-mythical. Incredible psychological transformations have taken place in other nonrevolutionary countries. The warlike Japanese and Germans have become the world's foremost traders, and the Jews the foremost warriors. Hereditary enemies like France and Germany have become close collaborators, and a United Europe seems in sight. Former imperial powers are learning to function as dynamic small countries. Tendencies toward affiliation and federation are concurrent with tendencies toward loosening of long-established unions. The nonrevolutionary world is a seething alembic in which nations are transmuted, and new entities synthesized.

The revolutionary countries seem stuck in the mud. When Communist Czechoslovakia tried to shake off its torpor it became self-evident that it had to join the nonrevolutionary world. There is fear of change in all revolutionary countries.

3

The spirit of an age is the product not of achievements and happenings but of the type of humanity that makes things happen.

It is vital to remember that, in the West, the passage from the management of men to the administration of things coincided with the transfer of power from traditional elites to the middle class. The ageless spirit of most of history is due to the fact that from the beginning of history until well into the first half of the nineteenth century events were shaped and dominated by elites of kings, nobles, soldiers, priests and intellectuals. The coming to power of the middle class in the middle of the nineteenth century mattered more than the coming of the machine. Had the machine age been inaugurated by aristocrats or intellectuals, the last hundred years would have had a different temper and spirit.

First Things, Last Things

To an elite, power means power over men. It cannot savor power by dominating nature, by moving mountains and telling rivers whither to flow. Even when, as in Soviet Russia, an elite sets in motion vast projects to tame and master nature, it uses these projects as a means for mastering and regimenting men. No elite would countenance, let alone promote, a state of affairs in which things happen of themselves, without command and obedience.

The middle class is the least elitist ruling class we know of. Not only is it wide open to all comers, but it aspires to a state of affairs in which things happen of themselves, and regulate themselves. Unlike any other ruling class, the middle class has found it convenient to operate on the assumption that if you leave people alone they will perform tolerably well; and under no other ruling class have common people shown such willingness to exert themselves to the utmost. It is this fabulously productive, more or less self-regulating chaos of a society that has given the modern age its singular spirit, and set it off from all preceding centuries. Regimentation and minute regulation are as ancient as civilization. Small wonder that elitists of every stripe—aristocrats, Marxists, Fascists, priests, power-hungry intellectuals—have viewed middle-class society and the modern age as abominations.

4

Just now the middle-class society is in deep trouble. Several paradoxes of the human condition have combined to turn its successes into critical failures. Affluence is showing itself to be a greater threat to social stability than poverty. The accelerating rate of change, though the change is mostly for the better, is upsetting and weakening traditions, customs, habits, routines—all the arrangements which make everyday life self-starting and self-regulating. At a time when miracles are becoming commonplaces, the commonplaces of everyday life can no longer be taken for granted. Finally, the education explosion is enormously increasing the number of people who want to live meaningful, relevant and important lives but lack the ability to attain relevance and significance by individual achievements.

To cope with these difficulties the middle class must learn how to contain anarchy, how to regulate and manipulate everyday life and, above all, how to concoct a faith, a philosophy, and a style of life to suit the needs of a noncreative horde hungering for meaningful, weighty lives. In short, in order to win, the middle class must lose itself. It must shape itself in the image of the elitists who hope and work for its destruction.

First Things, Last Things

There is much talk now of the death of an age and the birth of a new one. The stalwarts of the Now Generation claim to be the carriers of the new spirit. They say the generation gap is actually a gap between two ages different from, and incomprehensible to, each other. My hunch is that, whether the middle class resolves the present crisis or is pushed aside by new men, the age that is waiting for us around the corner will be not new but ancient. It will be an age preoccupied with the mastery of men—static and ageless despite its advanced technology.

Thus the indications are that the spirit of an age is not only a new phenomenon in history but a shortlived, one-time thing. The trajectory into which the Occident was catapulted over a hundred years ago is turning out to be a loop that curves back to where it started. And when we get back to the ancient, rutted highway of history we shall find that the revolutionary countries have arrived there before us, making good their boast that they are the wave of the future.

8

Thoughts on the Present

We of the present have a more vivid awareness of the tragic paradox central to the human condition than had any before us. It is not that we have experienced or seen greater evils. Incredibly monstrous as were the evils of the Stalin-Hitler decades, they have not appreciably affected social thought and practice. Our increased awareness has come from new revelations not about the nature of evil but about the nature of the good. No other generation has been made so poignantly conscious of the perils of doing good. We know that to set out to do good is to run the gauntlet of baffling, grotesque side effects. We know that the moment of greatest danger to a society is when it comes near realizing its most cherished dreams.

Enough has been said in preceding chapters about the

disintegration of values and the weakening of social discipline which come in the wake of widespread affluence. The legend of Adam's expulsion from Eden has for us a new poignancy: not even God Himself could cope with man in a paradisiacal existence. It was also in Eden that man first had truck with the devil. But more trying than the ordeal of affluence is the ordeal of justice. The ills and woes which beset our society at present and strain it to the breaking point were born of a concerted effort to right wrongs and do good: to give equality to the Negro, improve the lot of the poor, and throw open to all the gates of education and self-improvement.

Who would have dreamt that an unprecedented improvement in the lot of the Negro would result in burning and looting in cities; that the unprecedented affluence of the young would bring into being adolescent skid rows with adolescent whores, pimps, dope pushers, moochers and derelicts; that unprecedented opportunities for education would bring anarchy to places of learning? Whereas medical doctors when they prescribe a new drug warn the patient against dangerous side effects, our quacks of the body politic assume that their prescribed reforms can never go wrong.

We know now that in human affairs there is no certainty that good follows from good and evil from evil. As we enter the last third of the century it ought to be self-evident that when a society sets out to purge itself of iniquities and shortcomings it should expect the worst and gird itself for a crisis that will test its stability and stamina. A just society must strive with all its might to right wrongs even if righting wrongs is a highly perilous undertaking. But if it is to survive, a just society must be strong and resolute enough to deal swiftly and relentlessly with those who would mistake its good will for weakness.

2

It is questionable whether the Negro revolution can do much for the Negro. The Negro's future in this country will be determined by his ability to compete and excel. If the Negro cannot learn to strive and build on his own he will remain lowest man on the totem pole no matter how explosive his slogans and how extravagant his self-dramatization. Nevertheless, the Negro revolution is a fateful event because of its effect on non-Negro segments of the population. It is an illustration of the fact that the most important revolutions are those other people make for us.

The effect of the Negro revolution on the non-Negro young is as unexpected as it is puzzling. Why have the young so wholeheartedly adopted the Negro's way of life? The Negrification of the young will have profound and durable effects on language, sexual mores, work habits and the attitude toward drugs. Even the young white racists are Negrified and do not realize it.

Equally fateful is the effect of the Negro revolution on ethnic groups. Not only have Puerto Ricans, Mexicans and Indians been emboldened to use the Negro's tactics, but the entrance of the Negro into the mainstream of American life is bringing about a reversion of the process of amalgamation in the melting pot. Everywhere you look you can see some degree of ethnic crystallization. The fact that the WASP uppercrust has shown a tendency to conciliate Negro militants at the expense of those in the middle has caused the ethnics to lose faith in the Mayflower boys. A Linsky now running for office would not dream of changing his name to Lindsay.

The Negro is also bringing the policeman onto the political stage. Policemen are being elected mayors of large cities and, should disorder escalate, we may have a policeman running for President.

Finally, the Negro revolution is transplanting the South to the big cities, and there is a chance that the South will break out of its political isolation. A sophisticated Southern politician who has stripped himself of Confederate impedimenta can now run for national office and find a constituency in the hard-pressed, brooding white masses in most of the big cities.

3

What strikes one about the activist young is their lack of zest. Their obscenities are wooden, their insolence without a sparkle, and even their violence is trancelike. They dissipate without pleasure and are vain without a purpose. The revolution of the young is not against regimentation but against effort, against growth and, above all, against apprenticeship. They want to teach before they learn, want to retire before they work, want to rot before they ripen. They equate freedom with effortlessness, and power with instant satisfaction.

Never have the young taken themselves so seriously, and the calamity is that they are listened to and deferred to by so many adults. A society that takes its solemn adolescents seriously is headed for serious trouble. How humorless and laughable the solemn young! One realizes that one of the chief differences between an adult and a juvenile is that the adult knows when he is an ass while the juvenile never does. There is a link between seriousness and dehumanization. Is there anything more serious than a cow grazing in the pasture? The nonhuman cosmos is immersed in an ocean of seriousness. Man alone can smile and laugh.

The hope is often expressed that student activism may eventually lead to genuine educational reform, provided an exasperated public does not lose patience and over-react. Is such a hope justified? I remember how in 1964 when Savio and his Free Speech Movement pals started their revolution on the Berkeley campus I had the feeling that I was witnessing the Latin-Americanization of an American university. The politicization of universities has been for decades a fact of life below the Rio Grande. But I have still to hear anyone maintain that education and academic performance in Latin America have attained some sort of excellence not found in institutions of learning untouched by a student revolution.

We are also told that the young have a special talent for diagnosing the ills of our age. I doubt whether this is true. The young have a genius for discovering imagined grievances. It goes without saying that imagined grievances cannot be cured but they enable the young to evade those aspects of reality which do not minister to their self-importance. "The imagined ills," says Laurens Van Der Post, "enable them to avoid the proper burden that life lays on all of us."

It is true that present-day young are idealistic. But theirs is the easy idealism that condemns abuses and pushes aside any thought that would reveal the difficulties and complexities inherent in righting wrongs. They are not willing to do the hard work by which alone the world can be improved. Hearing what they say, and seeing what they do, one suspects that one of the main functions of the young's idealism is finding good reasons for doing bad things.

One has the impression that the young do not want to, or perhaps cannot, grow up. Our campuses have become dour, playless nurseries echoing with doctrinaire baby talk. You see six-foot babies clamoring for power and protesting against universities not having adequate arrangements for child care.

Here in San Francisco, as I watch the young with their bedrolls hitching rides and see them sprawled on the grimy sidewalks of Market Street and Haight-Ashbury, I am reminded strongly of the Great Depression. That the great affluence of the 1960s should have produced a phenomenon so similar to that produced by the Great Depression, only substituting juveniles for grownups, is one more striking absurdity of an absurd age.

Never has youth been face to face with more breathtaking opportunities and more deadly influences, and never before has character been so decisive a factor in the survival of the young. Nowadays a ten-year-old must be possessed of a strong character in order not to get irrevocably flawed and blemished. The road from boyhood to manhood has become sievelike: those without the right size of character slip into pitfalls and traps. The society of the young is at present almost as subject to the laws of sheer survival as any animal society. In the Bay Area you can see the young preyed upon by dope pushers, pimps, perverts and thugs. The supposedly most sheltered generation is actually the most exposed.

The present-day young do not seem to go anywhere yet they are impatient. They cannot bide their time because it is not the time of their growth. It seems doubtful whether a generation that clamors for instant fulfillment and instant solutions is capable of creating anything of enduring value. Instantness is a characteristic of the animal world, where action follows perception with the swiftness of a chemical reaction. In man, because of his rudimentary instincts, there is a pause of faltering and groping, and this pause is the seedbed of images, longings, forebodings and irritations which are the warp and woof of the creative process. Peter Ulich, in *The Human Career*, underlines the social significance of the pause: "Rarely is anything more important for the rise of civilization than the human capacity to put an interval between stimulus and action. For within this interval grow deliberation, perspective, objectivity—all the higher achievements of the reflective mind."

The creative flow is predicated on an inner gradient,

on the damming-up of impulses and cravings. It is of singular import that a measure of self-denial should be a factor not only in ethics but also in the creative process, and that, as suggested in Chapter 3, a free affluent society must become a creative society if it is to keep stable and orderly. Yet one wonders how acceptable such insights are to a generation indoctrinated with the belief that suppression of appetites is dangerous both psychologically and politically.

One also suspects that the young's exaggerated faith in spontaneity and inspiration is a characteristic of unstretched minds. Creative people believe in hard work. At the core of every genuine talent there is an awareness of the effort and difficulties inherent in any achievement, and the confidence that by persistence and patience something worthwhile will be realized. It needs great effort to make an achievement seem effortless.

4

A fateful characteristic of our violent age is the nonviolence, the incredible meekness, of the victims. Almost without exception, the social scientists are telling us that Americans are at present more violent than they were in the past. Yet anyone who observes the American scene in any big city with his own eyes knows that it is not so. The American man in the street is infinitely less pugnacious, less quarrelsome, and less ready to take offense than he was in the past. We used to fight in the streets, in saloons and on the job. Neighbors used to argue shrilly over the fence and often come to blows! But just now the great majority of Americans are afraid to open their mouths. They will not get into a fight no matter what you call them, and will not get involved even when they see people murdered before their eyes. They are afraid to get angry. The crucial, central fact about contemporary Americans is their timidity—their cowardice.

Thousands of peaceful Americans in city streets and ghettos, in suburbs and on campuses are meekly submitting to muggers, robbers and hoodlums, and to foulmouthed insults and threats. Few hit back or speak out loudly in outrage. The other day, at Berkeley, a class of 250 students was addressed by an intruding Negro student as motherfuckers and warned not to come to class next day or have their throats slit. The punk was not thrown out. The professor, a famous teacher, begged the intruder to leave the class. Would it have been overreaction had the class rushed the foul-mouthed punk and thrown him out? Was it sheer humaneness that kept the famous professor meek in the face of insults and threats?

Thoughts on the Present

The students and the professor were plainly afraid. When cowardice becomes a fashion its adherents are without number, and it masquerades as forbearance, reasonableness and whatnot.

Our sociologist quacks are warning us that violence is a symptom of a deep-seated social disease; that "it is the most dangerous error to treat symptoms and not get to the root causes of the disease itself." They deprecate the demand for law and order on the grounds that "those who raise it are not intelligent enough to comprehend fully any complex issue or else have something other in mind than the concern for public safety." In human affairs it is the shallow mind that refuses to deal with symptoms and is not awed by the mystery of the visible. Those who, when probing man's behavior, brush aside what's on the surface, and look for "root causes," are like those who, when peeling an onion, discard scale after scale, and look for an inner kernel.

At a recent convention of lawyers in Philadelphia speaker after speaker maintained that crime and violence are caused by poverty, ignorance and despair. The dean of the Yale Law School spoke against the prosecution of lawbreakers if their cause is worthy. Someone even suggested that persons engaged in violent dissent should be paid by the government for fighting against unjust laws. The whole tenor of the convention was that we must learn to live with violence until all ills have been cured, and our faulty institutions have been reformed.*

The evidence of our eyes tells us that violence is not the outer manifestation of some dark disorder in the cellars of the mind but the perverse highjinks of unruly punks who think they can get away with it. We have here a virulent form of juvenile delinquency on a large scale. Seventy-five percent of crimes in the streets are committed by adolescents under twenty-one, and the odds are five to one they won't get caught. (The odds are fourteen to one in stealing and nine to one in housebreaking.) The young thugs stalk older people like animals stalking their prey. They not only rob but brutally beat their victims. They do it for money but also for excitement. It needs swift, unrelenting justice to take the fun out of violence and make willful juveniles think twice before they let themselves go.

The unavoidable conclusion is that the unprecedented meekness of the majority is responsible for the increase in violence. Social stability is the product of an equilibrium between a vigorous majority and violent

* The only defender of law enforcement at this convention of American lawyers was an Englishman—John Passmore Widgery, Lord Justice of the Courts of Appeal in Great Britain. He pointed out that "anyone who thinks relief of poverty will bring a decrease in crime is in for some kind of disappointment." The greatest part of England's slums was razed by Hitler's bombs, and the welfare state has practically eliminated poverty, but there has been a steady increase in crime. "Can we ever rely on the worth of a cause in justifying disorder? My answer is a simple and emphatic negative. There should be no bargain with and no concession to those who would have it otherwise."

minorities. Disorder does not come from an increased inner pressure or from the interaction of explosive ingredients. There is no reason to believe that the nature of the violent minorities is now greatly different from what it was in the past. What has changed is the will and the ability of the majority to react.

It is hard to tell what causes the pervasive timidity. One thinks of video-induced stupor, intake of tranquilizers, fear of not living to enjoy the many new possessions and toys, the example of our betters in cities and on campuses who high-mindedly surrender to threats of violence and make cowardice fashionable.

We do not know what is ahead of us. It is hardly likely that the violent minorities will abruptly change their ways. There is a vague feeling that a day of wrath is waiting around the corner when the saturated resentment of the long-suffering majority crystallizes in retaliation. It is impossible to say when, where and how the reaction will come.

9

The Madhouse
of Change

After the Second World War I spent two years (1947–48) writing a small book on the nature of mass movements, which Harper later published under the title *The True Believer*. Those were two years of utmost concentration and absorption. Yet even as I was writing the book there was something tugging at my mind, making me wonder whether my attempt to make sense of the Stalin-Hitler decades would have relevance to what was taking place in the postwar world, particularly to the strange goings-on in Asia and Africa. On both continents several countries won independence from foreign rule and began to modernize themselves in a hurry. The struggle for independence was relatively brief, but the attempt at modernization became a hectic affair, which turned every country into a madhouse. Now, modernization is not an occult process. It requires the building of roads, factories, dams, schools and so on. Why should the accomplishment of such practical tasks require the staging of a madhouse?

I spent two decades groping for an answer. Almost everything I have written during the past two decades has dealt with some aspect of this problem. Every time I stumbled upon something which looked like an explanation I wrote an essay. I acted on the assumption that in this sort of problem all hunches and guesses are legitimate. It occurred to me, for instance, that modernization is basically a process of imitation—backward countries imitate advanced countries—and I wondered whether there might not be something bruising and antagonizing in the necessity to imitate a superior model. For the backward, imitation is an act of submission, and it is reasonable to expect that the sense of inferiority inherent in imitation should breed resentment. So I wrote an essay on "Imitation and Fanaticism," in which I suggested that the backward have to rid themselves of their feeling of inferiority, must demonstrate their prowess, before they will open their minds and hearts to all that the world can teach them. Most often in history it was the conquerors who learned willingly from the conquered rather than the other way around. There is therefore a kernel of practicalness in the attempt of a Nasser or a Sukarno to turn their people into warriors.

The Madhouse of Change

It is a fact that nations with a warrior tradition, such as the Japanese or the inheritors of Genghis Khan in Outer Mongolia, find modernization less difficult than nations of subjected peasants such as Russia and China. The essay also suggested that imitation is least impeded when we are made to feel that our act of imitation is actually an act of becoming the opposite of that which we imitate. Communism can be an effective agency for the transmission of Western achievements to backward countries because it convinces the backward that by modernizing themselves they are actually becoming the opposite of the capitalist model they imitate. Finally, I pointed out that we are most at ease when we imitate a defeated or dead model, and that the impulse of the imitators is to defeat or even destroy the model they imitate.

I also noticed that the present modernization of backward countries is directed not by businessmen or traditional politicians but by intellectuals, and I blamed the madhouse on them. I wrote several essays in which I tried to prove that unlike prosaic men of action the intellectual cannot operate at room temperature, that he pants for a world of magic and miracles, and turns practical tasks into holy causes and Promethean undertakings. I suggested that should intellectuals come to power in an advanced country it, too, would turn overnight into a madhouse.

2

The explanation which appealed to me most and to which I hung on longest was an unlikely one for an American. I became convinced that change itself is the cause of the madhouse; that change as such is explosive. It took me long to reach this conclusion. In this country change is familiar and acceptable. We seem to change homes, jobs, habits, friends, even husbands and wives, without much difficulty. Actually, through most of history change has been a rare phenomenon. Think of it: the technology perfected in prehistoric times served as a basis of everyday life down to the end of the eighteenth century. A sharp break occurred about 150 years ago between an immemorial static world and a world of ceaseless change. It is obvious, therefore, that change is far from being as natural and matter-of-fact as we imagine it to be. Moreover, an observant person will notice that even in this country change is never free of irritation and elements of fear. We adjust ourselves quickly to a new job or a new environment, but the moments of anxiety are there. And if we had to change our whole way of life, as people have to do in developing countries, we too would become upset and unbalanced.

The obvious fact is that we cannot prepare and fit

ourselves for the wholly new. We are all apprentices when we tackle the new; skill and experience count for little and may even be handicaps. It takes time before we adjust ourselves to a wholly new situation and fit in. In other words, drastic change turns a whole population into misfits, and misfits live and breathe in an atmosphere of passion. We used to think that revolution is the cause of change. Actually it is the other way around: revolution is a by-product of change. Change comes first, and it is the difficulties and irritations inherent in change which set the stage for revolution. To say that revolution is the cause of change is like saying that juvenile delinquency is the cause of the change from boyhood to manhood.

To understand what is going on in the developing countries we must know what it is that misfits need above all. They need self-confidence, which means plenty of opportunities for successful action, for asserting themselves and proving their worth. Where there are such opportunities, change is likely to proceed without convulsions and explosions. We have seen it happen in this country. From the middle of the last century to the First World War some thirty million Europeans came to this country. They were for the most part peasants torn from the warm communal life of small towns and villages and dumped almost overnight on a strange, cold continent. If ever there was a drastic change this was it. The immigrants went through an upsetting, irritating and painful experience. They were misfits in every sense of the word, ideal material for a revolution. Yet we had no upheaval. The immigrants adjusted themselves quickly to the new environment. Why? Because they had an almost virgin continent at their disposal and unbounded opportunities for individual advancement and self-assertion.

In most of the developing countries there are only the meagerest opportunities for the individual to do something on his own. Most of these countries are unimaginably poor, with debilitated populations living on the edge of subsistence. Some countries, like Indonesia, are rich in natural resources, but their governments do not countenance individual enterprise and self-assertion. You cannot see a Sukarno or even a Suharto government telling the people of Indonesia to come and get it the way America told the immigrants from Europe. Now, what do misfits do when they cannot win a sense of confidence and worth by individual effort? They reach out for substitutes. The substitute for self-confidence is faith, and the substitute for self-esteem is pride. Faith and pride in what? In a leader, a holy cause, a nation, a race. And it is easily seen that once you operate with faith and pride you are going to have the bedlam atmosphere of a madhouse.

3

It is remarkable that all the time I was playing with these explanations I failed to see something that was staring me in the face. I failed to see that staging a madhouse in the course of rapid modernization was not peculiar to backward countries in Asia and Africa. It was only recently that it dawned upon me that Europe, too, has been living in an apocalyptic madhouse staged by Germany and Russia as they set out to modernize themselves at breakneck speed. The nationalist, racialist and revolutionary movements and the great wars, which have convulsed the Occident during the past hundred years, were the by-product of a drastic change in the life of the European masses when millions of peasants were transformed into urban, industrial workers. Seen against this apocalyptic background, my explanation of the explosiveness of change as due to the creation of a state of unfitness seemed pale and inadequate. I began to feel that change does more than create misfits, that it affects deeper layers of the psyche. Considering how rare change has been through most of history it is legitimate to assume that change goes against human nature, that there is in man a built-in resistance to change. It is not only that we are afraid of the new. Deep within us there is the conviction that we cannot merely adjust to change, that we cannot remain our old selves and master the new; that only by getting out of our skins, by becoming new men, can we become part of the new. In other words, change creates an estrangement from the self and generates a need for a new identity and a sense of rebirth. And it depends on the way this need is satisfied whether change runs smoothly or is attended with convulsions and explosions.

Let us go back to the thirty million immigrants who were dumped on our shores and see what really happened to them. I said that the reason they had adjusted themselves so quickly to the new environment was that they found abundant opportunities for individual advancement. Is this all there was to it? Actually a whole lot more happened to them. The moment the immigrants landed on our shores America grabbed hold of them, stripped them of their traditions and habits, gave them a new diet and a new mode of dress, taught them a new language, and often gave them a new name. Here was a classical example of processing people into new men. Abundant opportunities for action by themselves could not have transformed the transplanted peasants so quickly and smoothly.

Immigration, then, is a potent agency of human transformation. It is, moreover, an agency the masses will resort to of their own accord whenever there is a drastic change in their way of life. It is significant that the rapid industrialization of Europe was attended not only by mass movements but also by mass migrations to the new world. Marx cursed the discovery of gold in California for cheating him of his foretold and prayed-for glorious revolution. He said it was the injection of gold from California which saved tottering Europe. Actually it was the discharge of thirty million immigrants to America which postponed Europe's apocalyptic dénouement.

It should be obvious, of course, that immigration can effect a human transformation only when it is to a foreign country. Internal migration cannot do it. Even now when you want to transform a Sicilian or a Spanish peasant into an industrial worker you can do it more effectively by transferring him to Germany or France than to Milan or Barcelona. The Sicilian peasant who goes to Milan is not automatically processed into a new man, and he is likely to satisfy his need for a sense of rebirth by joining the Communist party or some other mass movement. Immigration to a foreign country is a do-it-yourself way for the masses to attain a sense of rebirth. When they achieve this sense by joining a mass movement they avail themselves of a device staged for them by intellectuals. It is easy to forget that mass movements are the creation not of the masses but of the intellectuals. Now, what is likely to happen to a Sicilian peasant who becomes an industrial worker in Milan did happen to millions of European peasants who flocked to the cities of their native countries in the second half of the nineteenth century: they attained a sense of rebirth and a new identity by joining the nationalist and revolutionary movements staged for them by poets, writers, historians and scholars, and their adjustment to a new life became a convulsive and explosive affair which eventually shook the Occident to its foundations.

Mass movements play a twofold role in the process of change. First, they stage the drama of rebirth. By joining a mass movement we become members of a chosen people—saints, warriors or pioneers showing the way to the rest of mankind. Second, by fusing people into a compact, corporate body a mass movement creates a homogeneous, malleable mass that can be molded at will. We who have lived through the Stalin-Hitler decades know that one of the chief achievements of a mass movement is the creation of a population that will go through breathtaking somersaults at a word of command, and can be made to love what it hates and hate what it loves.

4

There is one drastic change which no society can avoid; namely the change from boyhood to manhood.

The Madhouse of Change

It is a difficult and painful change, and we all know its explosive by-product of juvenile delinquency. How do ossified, changeless societies weather this change? I was particularly interested in primitive, tribal societies which have remained unchanged for millennia. When I first started to look into this matter I had no idea what I would find. I happened to come upon a translation of Arnold Van Gennep's *The Rites of Passage*, and as I turned the pages I had the surprise of my life. There it was in black and white: the rites primitive societies stage to ease the boy's passage to manhood are the rites of death and rebirth. In the Congo boys at the age of fifteen are declared dead, taken into the forest and there given enough palm wine so that they pass out. The priest-magician watches over them until they come to. He then feeds them special food and teaches them a new language. During the rites of reintegration the boys have to pretend that they do not know how to walk, and that like newborn children they have to learn the gestures of everyday life. In several Australian tribes the boy is taken violently from his mother, who weeps for him. He is taken into the desert, where he is subjected to physical and mental weakening to simulate death. He is then resurrected to live like a man.

In modern societies, which have no rites of passage, the juvenile gropes his way to manhood on his own. He becomes an ideal recruit for mass movements. Indeed, the rapport between juvenile and mass movement is so striking—the two are so tailor-made for each other—that anyone, whatever his age, who joins a mass movement begins to display juvenile traits. This intimate linkage between juvenile and mass movement, and the fact that change readies people for mass movements, gave me a new view of the nature of change. Change, I realized, causes juvenilization; it turns a whole population into juveniles. It is as if the strain of change cracks the upper layers of the mind and lays bare the less mature layers. Another way of putting it is that people who undergo drastic change recapitulate to some degree the passage from childhood to manhood, and mass movements are in a sense the juvenile delinquency of societies going through the ordeal of change.

The juvenile, then, is the archetypal man in transition. There is a family likeness between juveniles and people who migrate from one country to another, or are converted from one faith to another, or pass from one way of life to another—as when peasants are turned into industrial workers, serfs into free men, civilians into soldiers, and people in backward countries are subjected to rapid modernization. Even the old when they undergo the abrupt change of retirement may turn, so to speak, into senile juveniles. Retired farmers and shopkeepers have made of Southern California a breeding ground of juvenile cults, utopias and movements.

The Madhouse of Change

5

In all my thinking about change America occupied a special place. I thought of it as a country with almost physiological adaptations to continuous, rapid change. Change with us was natural and normal—an expression of our dynamism. It was as Henry Ford said: "The only kind of stability we know in this country is change." But in 1963, while preparing a collection of my essays on change in backward countries, I began to feel that change has become one of America's problems.

As we have seen,* the Negro revolution has been inducing unanticipated changes in non-Negro segments of the population. But more significant is the fact that the Negro revolution has impaired America's singular faculty for taking change in its stride. Unlike the millions of European immigrants, the Negro millions have not been favored by chance and circumstances in their attempt to enter the mainstream of American life. In the light of what has been said in this chapter it is easy to see the handicaps which beset the Negro in his passage from inferiority to equality. Take the matter of *rebirth*. The fact that in this country the Negro is a Negro first and only secondly an individual puts the attainment of

* Pp. 101–103.

a sense of rebirth beyond his reach. No matter what the Negro individual achieves or becomes he remains a Negro first. Think of the demented absurdities Elijah Muhammad had to concoct in order to give the Negro some taste of rebirth.

Or take *immigration*. Millions of Negroes have migrated from the South to other parts of the country, but this mass migration has not helped the Negro to change himself. It was an internal migration, which, as we have seen,* cannot work a human transformation, and cannot endow people with a new identity. The Negro ghettos outside the South are a world of "nowhereness" and "nobodiness," where the groping for identity often assumes the aspects of a nightmarish masquerade.

Can *mass movements* do aught for the Negro? The answer is no. America is hard on mass movements. What starts out here as a mass movement ends up as a corporation or a racket. The Black Muslim movement is on the way to becoming a holding company of stores, farms and banks, while the civil-rights movement is largely an instrument in the hands of the Negro middle class to force its way into the privileged enclaves of American life. Used thus, the Negro revolution is not a movement but a racket. The Negro middle class has neither faith in nor concern for the Negro masses.

* P. 123.

The Madhouse of Change

In 1963 I had the feeling that the difficulty experienced by some twenty million Negroes in their passage to equality was effecting other types of change. I sensed that the crisis I saw gathering force before my eyes was basically an ordeal of change. Now, in 1970, it is generally recognized that America has joined the backward countries in the madhouse of change. Indeed, the Latin-Americanization of the universities, the Africanization of the big cities, the decline of efficiency in manufacturing and service, the incapacity to maintain the social plant in good repair, the tax-cheating rich and the swaggering intelligentsia are giving America the aspect of a backward country. But, whereas backward countries undergoing change usually think they know whither they are tending, America is just now completely in the dark about the future. Caught in a whirl of fantastically accelerated change we are beginning to wonder whether a society, or life itself, can thrive in an environment so lacking in continuity.

Things have been changing so rapidly during the 1960s that the present has almost ceased to exist. The vanishing of the present is having peculiar consequences. When the present is almost nonexistent, future and past too become blurred. The future is so immediate that one no longer waits for it. Hope turns into desire. At the same time, rapid change impairs memory—yesterday seems beyond recall. It is a state of affairs ideally suited to the inclinations of the adolescent. He contemptuously dismisses the fact that he has no past since the past is irrelevant. Nor can he see any sense in wasting his time preparing himself for the future. Tomorrow is now.

The vanishing of the present is hard on grownups. It devalues their experience, skills and convictions, and reduces them to the level of adolescents. Paradoxically, it is this blurring of the dividing line between grownups and the young that creates a generation gap. The young become arrogant in an age of not knowing, when the old are no longer sure of themselves, and growing up becomes meaningless. It is simply not true that equality between old and young breeds mutual love and respect.

We are also discovering that in our time of rapid change, though it is a time of widespread automation, nothing happens automatically. The vanishing of the present weakens the social automatism so essential to the functioning of a free society. Where everything is possible the familiar ceases to be self-evident. Everything has to be prompted and regulated.

We are up against the paradox that the post-industrial, super-modern age is becoming primitive and backward. You wonder what learned people mean when so many of them repeat the cliché that we have to modernize our institutions if they are to cope with a bewilderingly changing, modern society. The assumptions behind this cliché are so much taken for granted that they are never spelled out. It is assumed that in a whirling society nothing must remain stationary; that continuity is a drag that generates friction and heat. It is also assumed that the present brand of modernity is the opposite of the primitive. Actually, the trouble with our institutions is that they are, on the whole, too enlightened and civilized to hold their own in a social environment that is becoming increasingly primitive and savage. Moreover, there is no evidence that "modernized" institutions ease the flow of change. In Germany and Japan, where industrialization proceeded at breakneck speed, the political institutions were markedly feudal. In Britain, institutional continuity was a striking feature of the industrial revolution, and in this country political conservatism went hand in hand with unprecedented economic and social transformations. On the other hand, no one will maintain that the revolutionized institutions of Soviet Russia have smoothed the path of change. It is startling how little can be changed by total change. It can be argued that the sharp break with its past impeded Russia's modernization. When we break with the past we do not cast it off but swallow it. In Russia the renounced past, including that of Ivan the Terrible, became a conspicuous ingredient of Soviet life.

The changes that grow and endure are the changes

First Things, Last Things

sheltered by a strong framework of continuity. Later, when the new becomes a going concern, we can discard what we have carried over. We can act as total revolutionaries only when the revolution has already taken place.

71 72 73 10 9 8 7 6 5 4 3 2